Margaret Rizza

River of Peace

music for contemplative worship

Kevin Mayhew

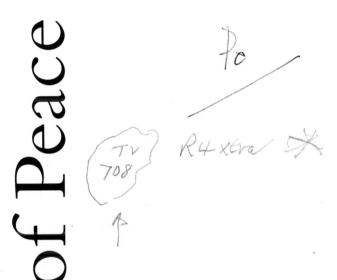

We hope you enjoy *River of Peace*. Further copies are available
from your local music shop or Christian bookshop.

In case of difficulty, please contact the publisher direct by writing to:

The Sales Department
KEVIN MAYHEW LTD
Buxhall
Stowmarket
Suffolk
IP14 3BW

Phone 01449 737978
Fax 01449 737834
E-mail info@kevinmayhewltd.com

Please ask for our complete catalogue of outstanding Church Music.

River of Peace is available as follows:

1400222 **Vocal score** includes the melody, keyboard, guitar and optional vocal parts

1490050 **CD** includes all fourteen pieces directed by Margaret Rizza

1480065 **Cassette** includes all fourteen pieces directed by Margaret Rizza

First published in Great Britain in 1999 by Kevin Mayhew Ltd.

© Copyright 1999 Kevin Mayhew Ltd.

ISBN 1 84003 469 6
ISMN M 57004 620 1
Catalogue No: 1400221

0 1 2 3 4 5 6 7 8 9

Cover design by Jaquetta Sergeant

Music Editors: Donald Thomson and Rachel Judd
Music setting by Donald Thomson

Printed and bound in Great Britain

Contents

	Page
Prayer for Peace	10
Come, my way	16
Song of the angels	21
Keep watch with me	36
Creator God	42
Inpoured Spirit	50
Hymn of St Patrick	54
Benedictus	56
As Joseph was a-walking	62
Sanctus Dominus	70
O magnum mysterium	79
Jesus, your heart is a womb	82
Gethsemane	86
Life of Christ renew me	96

Important Copyright Information

The Publishers wish to express their gratitude to the copyright owners who have granted permission to include their copyright material in this book. Full details are clearly indicated on the respective pages.

The **words** of *most* of the songs in this publication are covered by a **Church Copyright Licence** which allows local church reproduction on overhead projector acetates, in service bulletins, songsheets, audio/visual recording and other formats.

The **music** in this book is covered by the newly introduced 'add-on' **Music Reproduction Licence** issued by CCL (Europe) Ltd and you may photocopy the music and words of the songs in this book provided:

You hold a current Music Reproduction Licence from CCL (Europe) Ltd.

The copyright owner of the hymn or song you intend to photocopy is included in the Authorised Catalogue List which comes with your Music Reproduction Licence.

Full details of both the Church Copyright Licence and the additional Music Reproduction Licence are available from:

Christian Copyright Licensing (Europe) Ltd, PO Box 1339, Eastbourne, East Sussex, BN21 4YF. Tel: 01323 417711, fax: 01323 417722, e-mail: info@ccli.com, web: www.ccli.com.

Please note, all texts and music in this book are protected by copyright and if you do <u>not</u> possess a licence from CCL (Europe) Ltd, they may <u>not</u> be reproduced in any way for sale or private use without the consent of the copyright owner.

Foreword

Peace I bequeath to you, my own peace I give you,
a peace the world cannot give, this is my gift to you.

John 14:27

This third collection of contemplative music of chants, hymns and choral works was written over a period of six months – months which have been for me a time of reflection and pondering on the very nature of peace.

During this time many devastating and tragic things have happened in the world; one is confronted by injustice, unrest and division between peoples of many different countries where so often it is the innocent and the poor who suffer.

The international *Prayer for Peace* which I have set as a very simple hymn, is said daily at noon in many countries throughout the world and has been translated into more than forty languages. It expresses much of what peace is about; that it must first begin in our own hearts. Only then can it radiate out into the world.

For me the struggle for peace is not an easy option, but one which will cost not less than everything. It involves poverty of spirit and a letting go of those worldly things which make us feel strong but can be at the expense of others. There are also many things opposed to peace which influence us as we live out our lives in our competitive and materialistic, yet spiritually hungry, society.

These chants, hymns and choral pieces form a chain of prayer, a river which is calling us, drawing us, to strive for that peace which the world cannot give, whether it is, for example, through the anguish of *Gethsemane*, the mystery of *O magnum mysterium*, the justice and peace of *Song of the angels*, the deep stillness of *Inpoured Spirit*, or the transforming power of *Life of Christ*. Throughout the fourteen pieces there are these different aspects of prayer for seeking peace in our hearts and in our world.

If the music is used in parishes most of it can be sung and played according to the musical abilities and resources of the particular parish. The chants and hymns are infinitely expandable and can be used in many different ways.

I have so many people to thank who have helped me during these months of writing the music: my beloved family who very often have to cope with a hermit-like wife and mother; St Thomas' Music Group and the Church with whom I have shared many things and who are such an important part of the music-making; my publisher who has always given me so much support and encouragement, and the many people involved with the publishing and recording of this music; and the Christian Meditation Communities (WCCM) who over the years have become an intrinsic part of my life.

And so again my hope is that this music will be a way of prayer; a way to still our busy and distracted minds so that our hearts may be open to the healing and transforming work of this life-giving eternal Spirit who strengthens and empowers us to work for his Kingdom on earth. I pray that it will bear the fruit of peace.

MARGARET RIZZA

About the composer

Margaret Rizza [Lensky] studied at the Royal College of Music, London, and the National School of Opera, London, and completed her operatic training in Siena and Rome. She has sung at many of the world's leading operatic venues and under such conductors as Benjamin Britten, Igor Stravinsky and Leonard Bernstein. She was also a frequent broadcaster.

From 1977 to 1994 she taught singing and voice production at the Guildhall School of Music and Drama, London. She has trained and conducted several choirs, and is the founder of The Cameo Opera, The Cameo Singers and the St Thomas' Music Group.

Since 1983 she has dedicated herself to the work of spirituality and to the wider aspect of music in the community. She has led many retreats and days of prayer and is closely involved with the World Community for Christian Meditation (WCCM).

She now devotes herself to full-time composition, vocal and choral workshops, and to retreat-giving and days of prayer.

Her previous two collections, *Fountain of Life*, and *Fire of Love* are also available from Kevin Mayhew.

Singing these chants

You will find that in using this music most of it can be done very simply indeed by the smallest of groups, singing in unison, or it can be expanded to incorporate much larger forces who have more diverse musical resources at their disposal.

I would like to give some suggestions for both these groups but, having said this, they are only guidelines and in the end it is you who will decide. Do be adventurous and work on variety. It is lovely to hear the different voices being highlighted, sometimes male, sometimes female, sometimes solo, sometimes children's voices; and then to hear the different colours of the various instruments – all facets of God's life, love and beauty being revealed, poured out and manifested through our musical gifts.

There will naturally be more freedom of choice in the chants which can be as short as 2-3 minutes or as long as 8-10 minutes, but even in the other compositions much can be adapted to accommodate the various resources which you have available.

The following chant patterns are the ones used for the recording of *River of Peace*, but as I have pointed out, there are many different ways of working the chants, and in the end it will be your choice.

'PRAYER FOR PEACE' CHANT PATTERN

1. Trumpet – theme; organ, cello
2. Unison voices
3. SATB voices unaccompanied
4. SATB; trumpet – var., organ, cello into last-time bars

'COME MY WAY' CHANT PATTERN

1. Verse 1: solo voice
2. Verse 1: sopranos, ATB hum.
3. Verse 1: SATB; organ, cello and guitar – continue
4. Instrumental trio: oboes 1 & 2 – var. 1, flute – var. 3
5. Verse 2: unison voices; cello – var. 1
6. Verse 2: SATB; cello
7. Instrumental duet: violin – var. 4, cello – var. 1
8. Verse 3: SATB; recorder duet
9. Verse 3: SATB with soprano descant; violin – var. 3
10. SATB into last-time bars

SONG OF THE ANGELS

Choir, organ, cello, guitar, oboes 1 & 2, clarinet

'KEEP WATCH WITH ME' CHANT PATTERN

1. Organ and guitar – continue
2. Unison voices
3. SATB 1
4. SATB 2; organ accomp. 2, cellos join basso continuo
5. SATB 1 'ah'/hum; clarinet – var., organ accomp. 1, cello – b.c. 1
6. SATB 1 'ah'/hum; oboe – var. 1, organ accomp. 1, cello – b.c. 2
7. SATB 2; organ accomp. 2, cello – b.c. 2
8. SATB 1 'ah'; flute duet; organ accomp. 1, cello – b.c.1
9. SATB 1 'ah'; cello – var. 1, violin – var. 3
10. SATB 2 with soprano descant into last-time bars; organ – accomp. 1, cello – b.c. 2

'CREATOR GOD' CHANT PATTERN

1. Trumpet – theme; organ and cello – continue
2. Verse 1: unison voices, women sing 8 bars then men sing 8 bars
3. Verse 1: SATB (*pp*); clarinet – var. 1
4. Verse 2: 4 men sing 8 bars then 4 women sing 8 bars while SATB sing 'ah' or hum; organ and cello tacet
5. SATB singing 'ah'; violin – var. 2 with cello duet; organ and cello continue
6. Verse 3: unison voices
7. Verse 4: SATB into last-time bars

'Inpoured Spirit' chant pattern

1. Organ and guitar – continue
2. Voices trio – Altos on 1; Sopranos join on 2 (duet); Men join on 3 (trio)
3. Unison voices on 1 of trio; cello – var. 1
4. Unison voices on 1 of trio; violin – var. 4
5. Voices trio (A, S, Men)
6. Unison voices on 1 of trio; oboes 1 & 2 – var. 3
7. SATB into last-time bars; flute duet – var. 5

Hymn of St Patrick
SATB voices unaccompanied

'Benedictus' chant pattern

1. Flute – theme; organ – continue throughout
2. Sopranos
3. SATB voices; cello and guitar join
4. SATB voices; trumpet – var. 2
5. Verses 1 & 2: cantors
6. SATB hum; oboe – var. 1
7. SATB hum; violin – var. 3
8. SATB 'ah'; cello – var. 1
9. SATB 'ah'; clarinet – var. 3
10. Verses 3 & 4: cantors
11. SATB voices; flute – var. 2; oboe – var. 1
12. SATB voices with soprano descant into last-time bars; trumpet – var. 2, oboe – var. 1

'As Joseph was a-walking' chant pattern

1. Solo voice unaccompanied
2. Verse 2: 4-6 sopranos sing words while SATB hum
3. Verse 3: SATB voices, the sopranos divide on the 'lullaby' parts; guitar and cello

'Sanctus Dominus' chant pattern

1. Introduction – organ, then continue
2. Oboe 1 – 1 of var. 1
   Oboe 2 – 2 of var. 1 (duet)
   Clarinet – 3 of var. 1 (trio)
3. SATB voices; cello joins and continues
4. SATB background; flute duet
5. SATB voices, semi-chorus
6. SATB voices, semi-chorus; clarinet, oboes 1 & 2

O magnum mysterium (for female voices)
Soprano and Alto voices

'JESUS, YOUR HEART IS A WOMB' CHANT PATTERN
1. Solo voice; organ
2. SATB voices; organ and cello

'GETHSEMANE' CHANT PATTERN
1. Cello – theme; organ continue throughout
2. Unison voices; cellos join
3. Unison voices – background; oboe – var. 1
4. Unison voices – background; violin – var. 3
5. Verse 1: cantors
6. Unison voices – background; cello – var. 1
7. SATB voices; oboe – var. 1; clarinet – var. 2 duet
8. Verse 2: cantors
9. SATB 'ah'; clarinet – var. 4
10. SATB 'ah'; flute duet – var. 5
11. Verse 3: cantors
12. SATB 'ah'; oboe, clarinet, trumpet trio
13. Verse 4: cantors
14. SATB voices, soprano variation; clarinet and trumpet – var. 8
15. SATB voices into last-time bars; trumpet

'LIFE OF CHRIST RENEW ME' CHANT PATTERN
1. Introduction – organ and guitar, then continue
2. Verse 1: unison voices; cello join
3. Verse 1: SATB voices; cello – var. 1 (pizzicato arpeggios)
4. Clarinet – var; guitar – tacet
5. Verse 2: unison women's voices; violin – var. 3, guitar joins
6. Verse 2: women sing in harmony unaccompanied; organ and cello tacet
7. Flute duet; organ and cello continue
8. Verse 3: unison men's voices
9. Verse 3: men's voices (trio); cello – var. for men's verse; organ and guitar tacet
10. Verse 4: SATB voices; flute and oboe – duet 2
11. Verse 4: SATB voices; descant sopranos
12. Verse 5: SATB voices; all instruments on appropriate lines

The instrumental parts given within this score are intended to be interchangeable to enable you to make the best use of the available resources. Parts for C instruments may be played by either flute, oboe, violin or recorder; parts for B♭ instruments by clarinet, soprano/tenor saxophone or trumpet; parts for E♭ instruments by E♭ horn or alto/baritone saxophone and parts for bass clef instruments by cello, bassoon or double bass.

PRAYER FOR PEACE

Text: Prayer for Peace
Music: Margaret Rizza

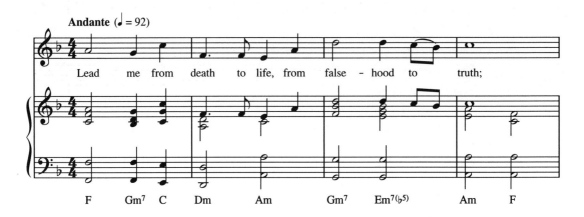

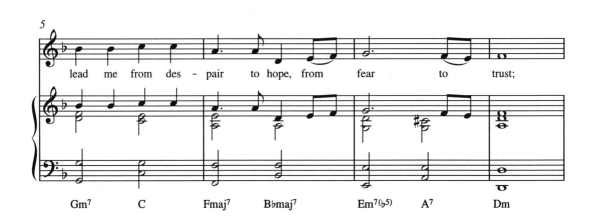

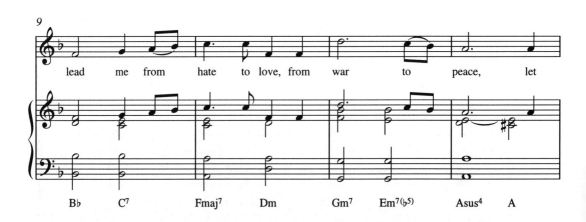

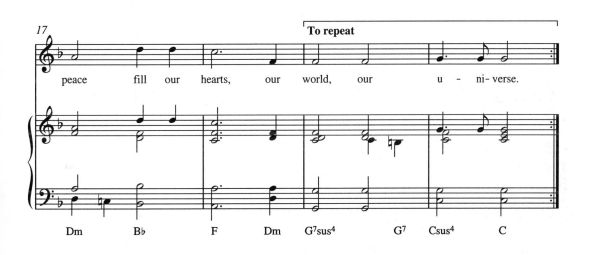

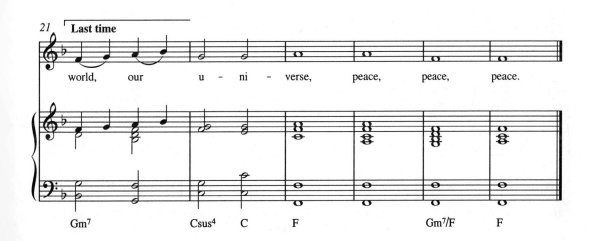

MIXED VOICES

Lead me from death to life, from false-hood to truth; lead me from des-

pair to hope, from fear to trust; lead me from hate to love, from

war to peace; let peace fill our hearts, our world, our

To repeat

u-ni-verse, let peace fill our hearts, our world, our u-ni-verse.

Last time

world, our u-ni-verse, peace, peace, peace.

INSTRUMENTAL PARTS

C INSTRUMENTS

Theme

Variation into last-time bars

Bb INSTRUMENTS

Theme

Variation into last-time bars

BASS CLEF INSTRUMENTS

COME, MY WAY

Text: George Herbert (1593-1633)
Music: Margaret Rizza

2. Come, my light, my feast, my strength;
   such a light as shows a feast.
   Such a feast as mends in length,
   such a strength as makes his guest.

3. Come, my joy, my love, my heart;
   such a joy as none can move.
   Such a love as none can part,
   such a heart, as joys in love.

Last time

1. Come, my way, my truth, my life; such a way, as gives us breath.

Such a truth, as ends all strife: such a life as kill - eth death.

Come, my joy, my love, my heart; such a love as none can part.

Soprano Descant for verse 3

Come, my joy, my love, my heart, such a joy as none can move;

such a love as none can part; such a heart, as joys in love.

Come, my joy, my love, my heart, such a love as none can part.

INSTRUMENTAL PARTS
C INSTRUMENTS

Variation 1: Duet for C Instruments

Variation 2

Variation 3
May be played with Variation 1 to make a Trio

Variation 4

Variation 5
Duet for C instruments

Bb INSTRUMENTS

Duet for Bb Instruments

8va ad lib.

Variation 2

Variation 3

BASS CLEF INSTRUMENTS

Basso Continuo

Variation 1

SONG OF THE ANGELS

Text: Howard Thurman (1900-1981)
Music: Margaret Rizza

When the song of the an-gels is stilled, when the star in the sky is gone.

When the kings and prin-ces are home,

when the shep-herds are back with their flocks.

E⁷sus⁴
Capo 2 D⁷sus⁴

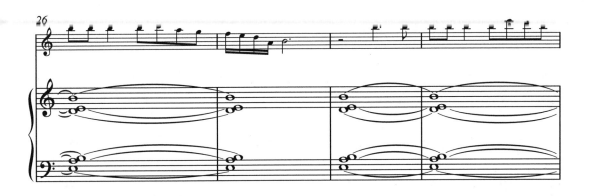

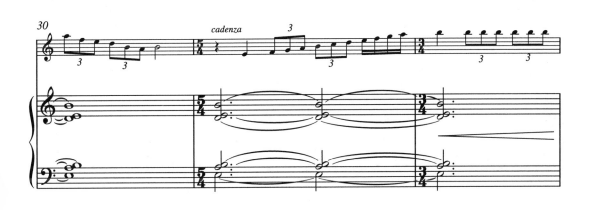

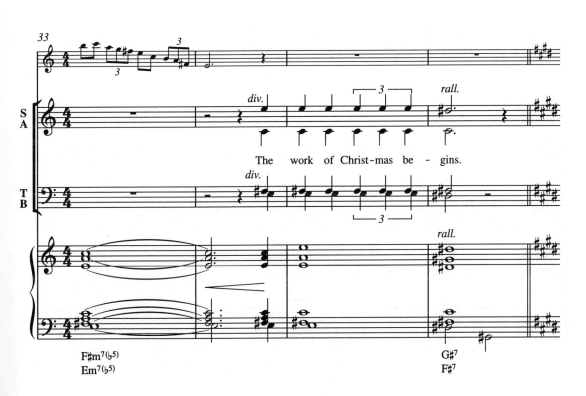

The work of Christ-mas be - gins.

F#m7(b5)
Em7(b5)

G#7
F#7

23

hun - gry,

the

to re-lease the pris - 'ner,

F#m⁷
Em⁷

B
A

Emaj⁷
Dmaj⁷

work of Christ - mas be - gins,

the work of Christ - mas be -

Fm⁷⁽♭⁵⁾
E♭m⁷⁽♭⁵⁾

B
A

F#⁷sus⁴
E⁷sus⁴

F#⁷
E⁷

gins; to re-build the na-tions, to bring

B   E   A   Amaj⁷   F♯m
A   D   G   Gmaj⁷   Em

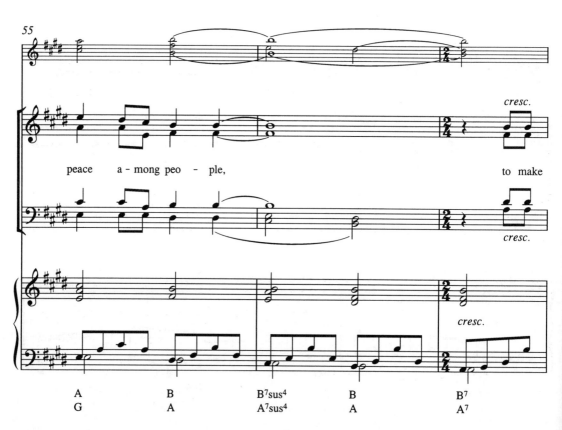

peace a-mong peo - ple, to make

cresc.

A   B   B⁷sus⁴   B   B⁷
G   A   A⁷sus⁴   A   A⁷

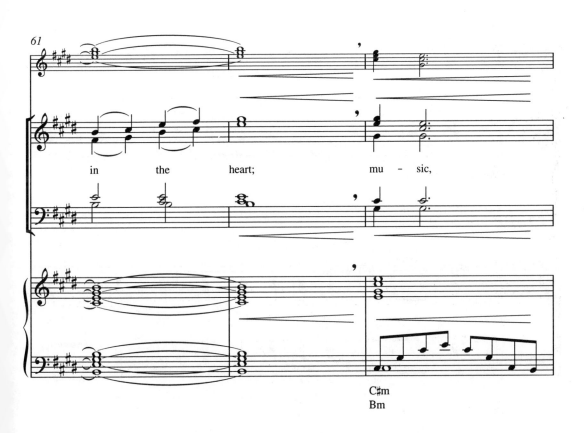

mu - sic, mu - sic in the heart. The

Amaj⁷   F♯m⁷   E   B⁷sus⁴   B⁷
Gmaj⁷   Em⁷   D   A⁷sus⁴   A⁷

Meno mosso

work of Christ-mas be - gins, when the song of the an - gels is

Guitar
tacet

still'd, when the star in the sky is gone, when the

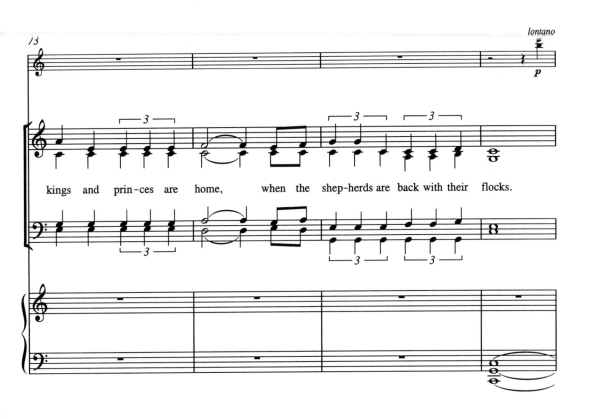

kings and prin-ces are home, when the shep-herds are back with their flocks.

The work of Christ-mas be - gins.

INSTRUMENTAL PARTS

C INSTRUMENTS

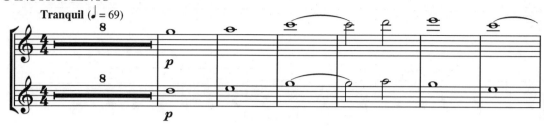

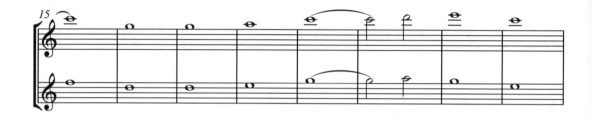

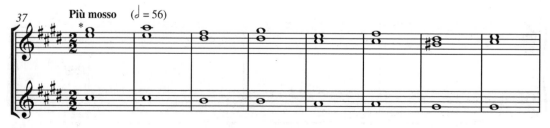

Take either part.

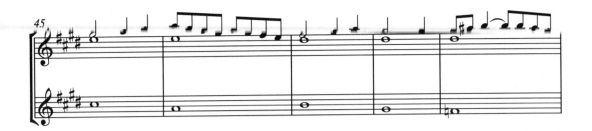

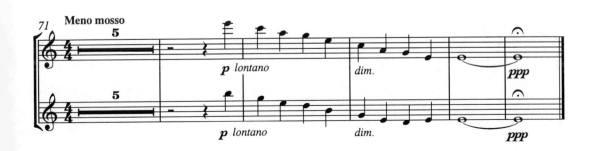

(**Men:** shepherds are back with their flocks.)

BASS CLEF INSTRUMENTS

KEEP WATCH WITH ME

Text: Traditional
Music: Margaret Rizza

MIXED VOICES

Harmony 1

S A: Keep watch with me, pray with me and do not be a-fraid; keep

watch with me, pray with me and do not be a-fraid; keep

Last time

watch with me, pray with me, do not be a-fraid.

Harmony 2

Keep watch with me, pray with me and do not be a - fraid; keep
watch with me, pray with me and do not be a - fraid; keep

Last time

watch with me, pray with me, do not be a - fraid.

Soprano Descant for Final Chant

Keep watch with me, pray with me and do not be a -
fraid; keep watch with me, pray with me and do not be a -
fraid; keep watch with me, pray with me, do not be a - fraid.

INSTRUMENTAL PARTS

C INSTRUMENTS

Bb INSTRUMENTS
Variation 1

BASS CLEF INSTRUMENTS
Basso Continuo 1

Last time

Basso Continuo 2

Last time

Variation 1

CREATOR GOD

Text and Music: Margaret Rizza

To next verse · Last time

14

full - ness, cre - a - tor God, you are there.   there.

Em⁷   D   Em⁷   Asus⁴ A   D   Bm

Intro ✓

18

ten.

In the love that is e - ter - nal, cre - a - tor God, you are there.

ten.

D   Bm   Em⁷   D   Em⁷   A⁹sus⁴ A⁷   D

2. In the homeless and the hungry,
   in the broken and the lonely,
   in the grieving of your people,
   creator God, you are there.
   In the tears and in the heartache,
   in the love through which we serve you,
   in the anguish of the dying,
   creator God, you are there.

3. In our hearts and in our thinking,
   in the longing and the dreaming,
   in the yearning of our heartbeat,
   creator God you are there.
   In the love for one another,
   in the sharing of our being,
   in receiving and forgiving,
   creator God, you are there.

4. In our joys, our hopes, our healing,
   in awakening to revealing,
   in your call and our responding,
   creator God, you are there.
   In our prayer and in our service,
   in our praise and in our worship,
   in your love that is eternal,
   creator God, you are there.

43

MIXED VOICES

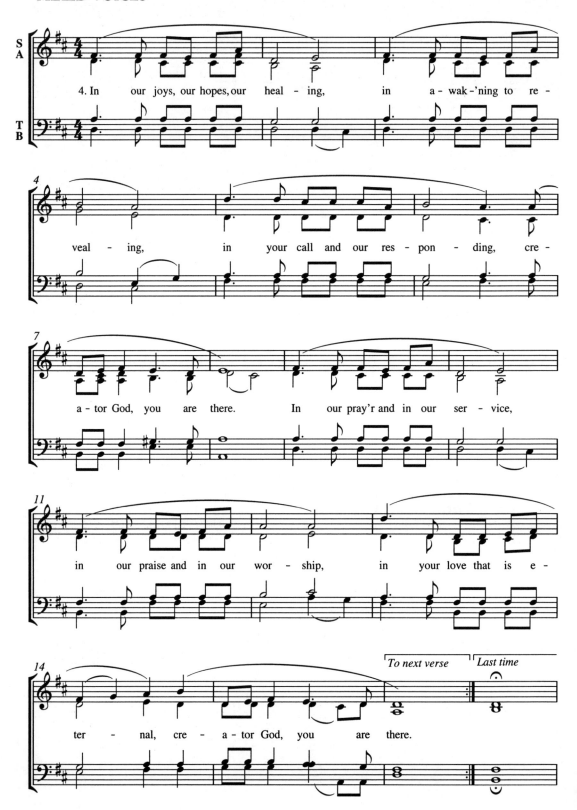

4. In our joys, our hopes, our heal - ing, in a - wak -'ning to re -
veal - ing, in your call and our res - pon - ding, cre -
a - tor God, you are there. In our pray'r and in our ser - vice,
in our praise and in our wor - ship, in your love that is e -

To next verse *Last time*

ter - nal, cre - a - tor God, you are there.

VOCAL VARIATIONS

Soprano descant for last verse

In the love that is e - ter - nal, cre - a - tor God, you are there.

SATB variation (with melody above)

'Ah' or Hum

INSTRUMENTAL PARTS

C INSTRUMENTS

Variation 2

B♭ INSTRUMENTS

Theme

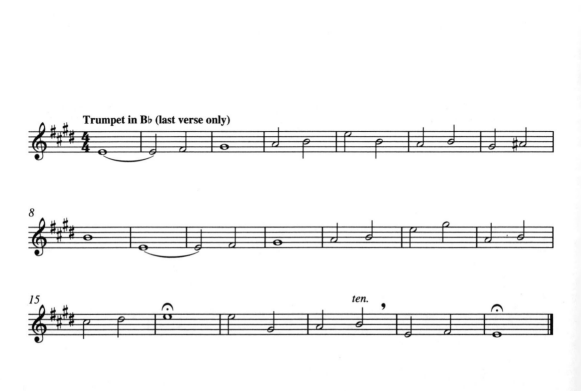

BASS CLEF INSTRUMENTS

Basso continuo

Duet with C instrument (Variation 2)

INPOURED SPIRIT

Text: Pamela Hayes
Music: Margaret Rizza

MIXED VOICES

51

VOCAL VARIATIONS

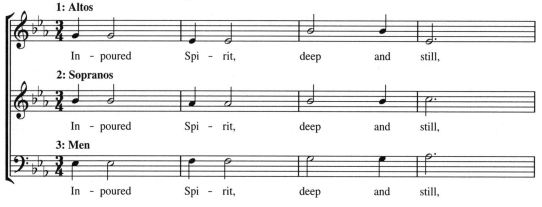

INSTRUMENTAL PARTS
C INSTRUMENTS

Variation 4

Variation 5: Duet for C Instruments
(2 repetitions of Chant)

BASS CLEF INSTRUMENTS

Basso Continuo

To repeat | Last time

Variation 1

Variation 2

HYMN OF ST PATRICK

Text: from 'The Hymn of St Patrick' trans. Cecil Frances Alexander (1818-1895)
Music: Margaret Rizza

BENEDICTUS

Text: Traditional
Music: Margaret Rizza

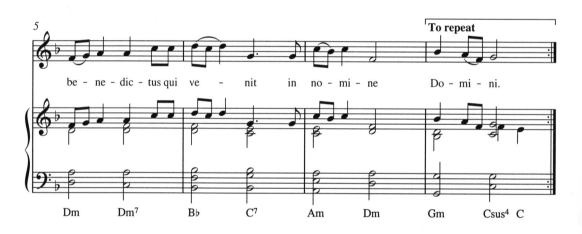

MIXED VOICES

Be - ne - dic - tus qui ve – nit in no - mi - ne Do - mi – ni,

To repeat

be - ne - dic - tus qui ve – nit in no - mi - ne Do - mi - ni.

Last time

Do - mi - ni, in no - mi - ne Do – mi – ni.

CANTOR
Verse 1

1. Bles-sed are the poor in spi-rit, for theirs is the king-dom of hea - ven;

bles-sed are those who mourn for they shall be com-for-ted.

Verse 2

2. Bles-sed are the meek, for they shall in-he-rit, for they shall in-he - rit the earth;

Over for verses 3 and 4

bles-sed are those who hun - ger and thirst, for what is right: they shall be sa-tis-fied.

Verse 3

3. Bles - sed are the mer - ci - ful, for they will be shown mer - cy;

bles - sed are the pure in heart, for they shall see God.

Verse 4

4. Bles-sed are the peace - ma -kers, for they shall be called the chil-dren of God;

bles-sed the per- se- cu-ted for righ -teous- ness' sake, for theirs is the king-dom of hea - ven.

Choral Accompaniment for Instrumental Variations

S
A

'Ah' (or Hum)

T
B

Soprano Descant for Final Chant

Ah,   ah,

ah,   ah,   in no - mi - ne Do - mi - ni.

58

INSTRUMENTAL PARTS

C INSTRUMENTS

Eb INSTRUMENTS

Variation 1

5

Variation 2

5

BASS CLEF INSTRUMENTS

Basso Continuo

7

To repeat | Last time

Variation 1

5

AS JOSEPH WAS A-WALKING

Carol in Gaelic mode

Text: from Anon. 14th century
Music: Margaret Rizza

* SIMPLE VERSION

Andante (♩ = 63)

1. As Jo-seph was a-walk-ing he heard an an-gel sing: this night shall be born our

hea - ven-ly King. He nei-ther shall be born in hou-sen nor in hall, nor

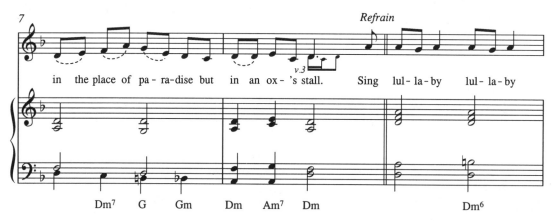

in the place of pa-ra-dise but in an ox-'s stall. Sing lul-la-by lul-la-by

* See page 65 for Choral Version

2. He neither shall be clothed in purple nor in pall,
   but all in fair linen as were babies all.
   He neither shall be rocked in silver nor in gold,
   but in a wooden cradle that rocks on the mould.

3. He neither will be guarded by weapons or by walls,
   he came as a saviour, so frail and so small.
   He neither shall be christened in white wine nor in red,
   but with spring water with which we all are christened.

AS JOSEPH WAS A-WALKING

Carol in Gaelic mode
Text: from Anon. 14th century
Music: Margaret Rizza

* CHORAL VERSION

Andante (♩ = 63)
Solo or Unison

1. As Jo - seph was a - walk - ing he heard an an - gel sing: this

night shall be born our hea - ven - ly King. He nei - ther shall be born in

hou - sen nor in hall, nor in the place of pa - ra - dise but in an ox - 's stall. Sing

lul - la - by lul - la - by lul - la - by ba - by. Sing lul - la - by lul - la - by

Sopranos

lul - la - by ba - by, ba - by lul - la - by ba - by. 2. He

a tempo
nei - ther shall be cloth - ed in pur - ple nor in pall, but all in fair li - nen

'Ah' or Hum

* See page 62 for Simple Version

as were ba-bies all. He nei-ther shall be rock-ed in sil-ver nor in gold, but

Refrain

in a wood-en cra - dle that rocks on the mould. Sing lul-la-by, lul-la-by,

lul-la-by ba-by, sing lul-la-by, lul-la-by, lul-la-by ba-by,

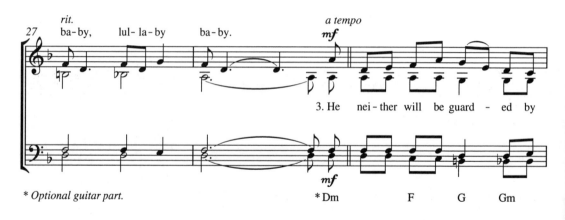

rit.   *a tempo*
ba-by, lul-la-by ba-by.   *mf*

3. He nei-ther will be guard - ed by

mf

* Optional guitar part.   *Dm   F   G   Gm

weapons or by walls; he came as a sa-viour, so frail and so small. He

Dm Edim Dm F C Dm G Dm

nei-ther shall be chris-ten-ed in white wine nor in red, but with spring wa-ter with

Bb Edim Am Dm G Dm Dm⁷ G Gm

Refrain

S

which we all were chris-ten-ed. Sing lul-la-by, lul-la-by, lul-la-by ba-by, sing

A

which we all were chris-ten-ed. Sing lul - la - by,

T
B

which we all were chris-ten-ed. Sing lul - la - by,

For rehearsal only

Dm C Dm Bm⁷⁽ᵇ⁵⁾ Bbmaj⁷ Em⁷⁽ᵇ⁵⁾ Dm

* *Before this point, the accompanist should follow the printed vocal parts.*

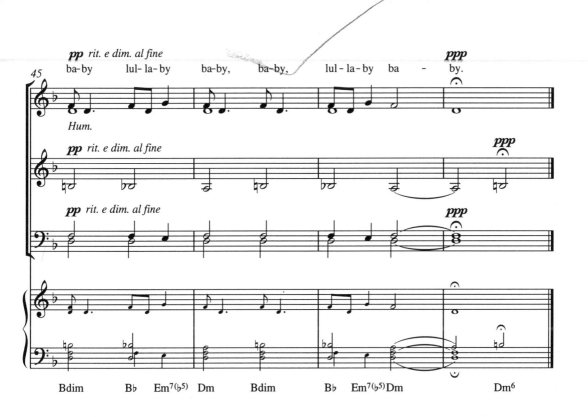

INSTRUMENTAL PARTS

Optional Cello part to accompany verse 3

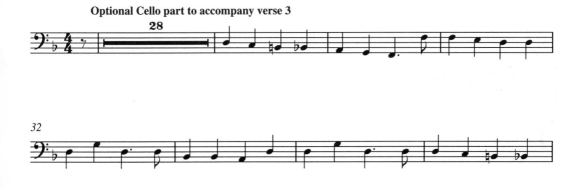

SANCTUS DOMINUS

Text: Traditional
Music: Margaret Rizza

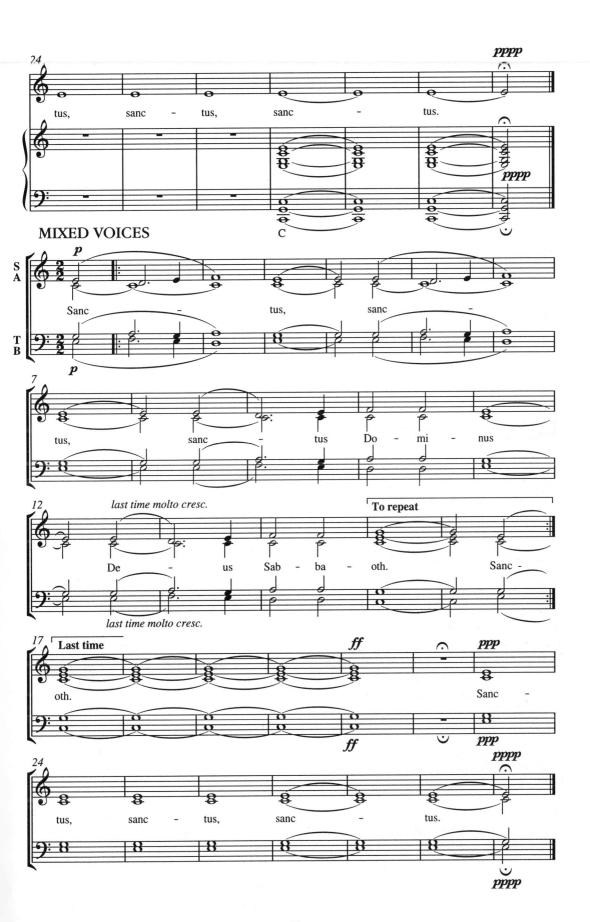

MIXED VOICES

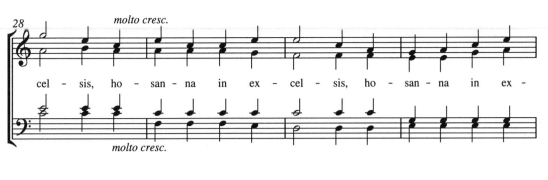

cel - sis, ho - san - na in ex - cel - sis, ho - san - na in ex -

cel - sis, ex - cel - sis, ex - cel - sis. Sanc -

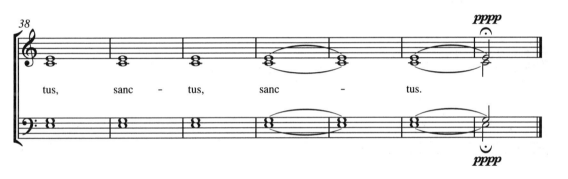

tus, sanc - tus, sanc - tus.

INSTRUMENTAL PARTS

C INSTRUMENTS

Variation 1: add a part on each repetition

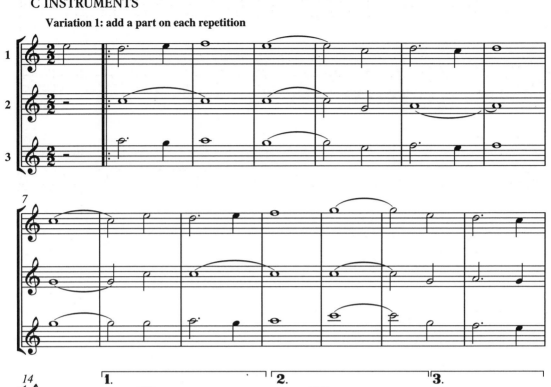

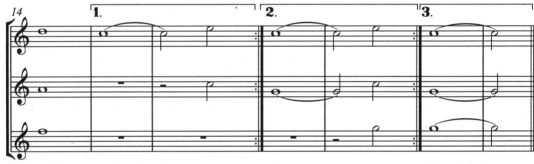

Variation 2: Solos or Duet

Final Variation: Trio for C Instruments

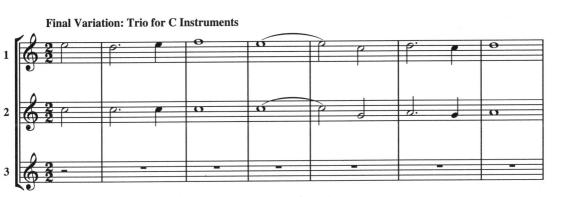

Bb INSTRUMENTS

Variation 1: add a part on each repetition

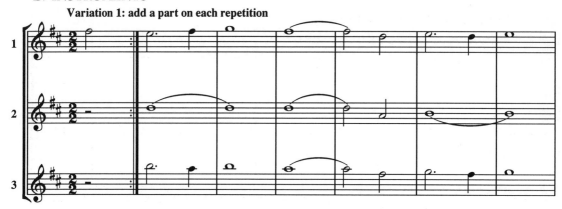

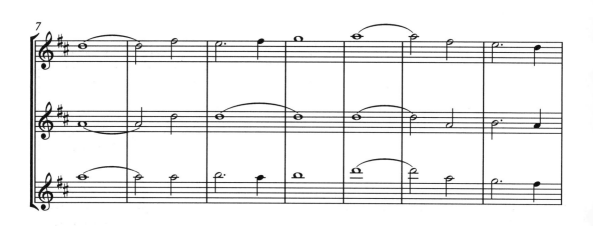

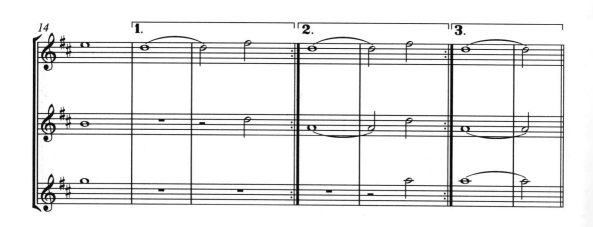

Final Variation: Trio for B♭ Instruments

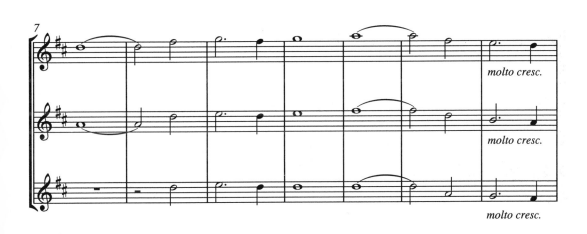

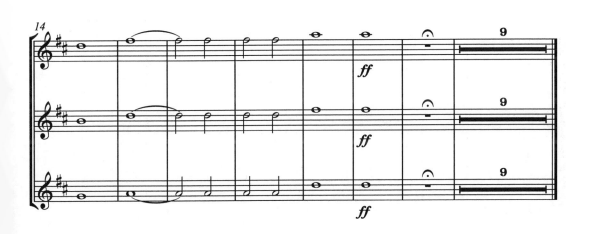

O MAGNUM MYSTERIUM

Text: from the Christmas Vigil (Year A)
Music: Margaret Rizza

Translation: O Great Mystery, and wondrous Sacrament, that living beings should see the Lord
born and lying in a manger: blessed is the Virgin whose womb was worthy
to bear Lord Christ. Blessed Mary.

gra - ti - a ple - na Do - mi - nus te - cum.

gra - ti - a ple - na Do - mi - nus te - cum.

Be -

Be -

a - ta, be - a - ta, be - a - ta.

a - ta, be - a - ta, be - a - ta.

81

JESUS, YOUR HEART IS A WOMB

Text: Pamela Hayes
Music: Margaret Rizza

MIXED VOICES

Je-sus, your heart is a womb, hold-ing our hu-ma-ni-ty,

woun-ded in fra-gi-li-ty. Je-sus, your heart is a gift: the

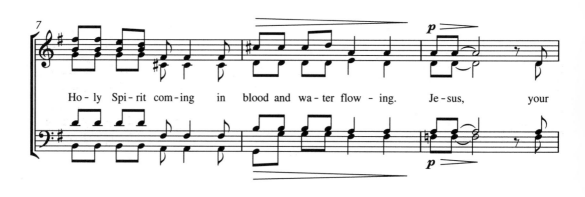

Ho-ly Spi-rit com-ing in blood and wa-ter flow-ing. Je-sus, your

heart is a wound o-pen to my-ste-ry: God in the Tri-ni-ty.

Je-sus, your heart is a flame en-kind-ling our com-pas-sion, cast-ing

fire u-pon the earth.   fire u-pon the earth.   Je-sus, your heart is a

womb;   Je-sus, your heart is a gift,   Je-sus, your heart is a

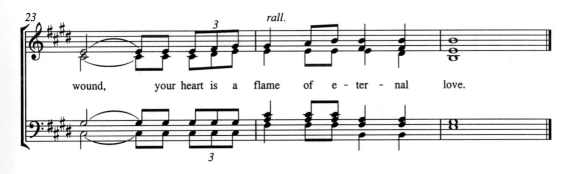

wound,   your heart is a flame of e - ter - nal love.

GETHSEMANE

Text: adapted from Matthew 26:36-8
Music: Margaret Rizza

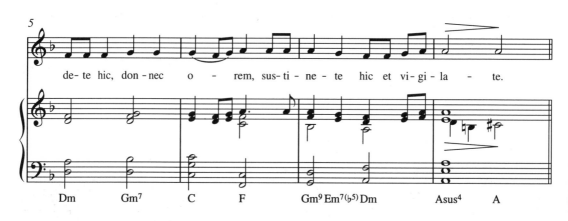

MIXED VOICES

Translation: My soul is ready to die with sorrow.
Sit down here while I go to pray.
Stay here and keep watch.

Final Descant before the CODA

Soprano (Semi-chorus)

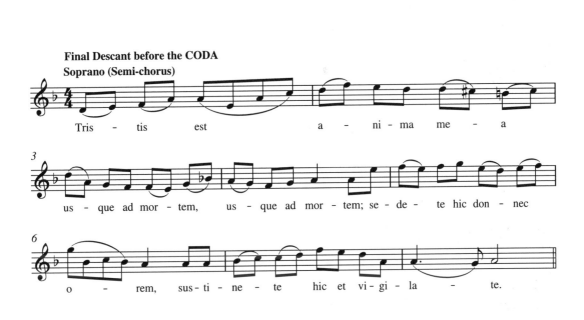

Tris - tis est a - ni - ma me - a

us - que ad mor - tem, us - que ad mor - tem; se - de - te hic don - nec

o - rem, sus - ti - ne - te hic et vi - gi - la - te.

Choral Accompaniment to Instrumental Variations

'Ah' or Hum

CANTORS

Narrator: Soprano, Alto or Tenor; Jesus: Bass or Baritone

Verse 1

Je-sus took with him Pe-ter, James and John. He said to them: 'My soul is stric-ken with a grief like death; wait here with me, stay a-wake with me, keep watch while I pray. My soul is stric-ken with a grief like death.'

Verse 2

Je-sus walked a lit-tle way and fell to the ground and prayed: 'My Fa-ther, if it is pos-si-ble, let this cup pass me by. But not what I want, but what you want; my Fa-ther, let it be as you want.'

Verse 3

Je-sus came back to his dis-ci-ples and found them sleep-ing. He said to Pe-ter: 'Could you not stay a-wake and pray here with me? Keep watch and pray you will not fall in-to temp-ta - tion; the

* Take either part

Spi - rit is will - ing but the flesh is weak.'

Verse 4

Twice a - gain Je - sus left his dis - ci - ples and went back to pray: 'My

Fa - ther, let this cup pass me by, but your will be done;' he

came back to find his friends sleep - ing and wa - king them, he said: 'The

hour has come, let us go, my be - tray - er is close at hand'.

CODA
C or B♭ Instrument

Tris - tis est a - ni - ma me - a, tris - tis est

INSTRUMENTAL PARTS
C INSTRUMENTS

Trio for C Instruments

B♭ INSTRUMENTS

Variation 1
Trumpet

Variation 2
Trumpet

Variation 3
Clarinet

8va ad lib.

Trio for Bb Instruments

BASS CLEF INSTRUMENTS

Introduction: theme

LIFE OF CHRIST RENEW ME

Text and Music: Margaret Rizza

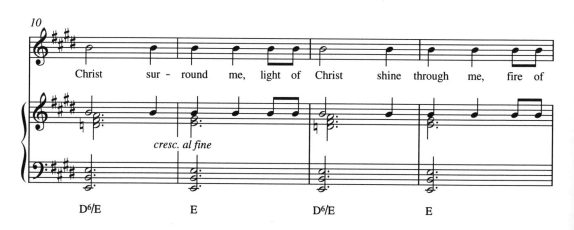

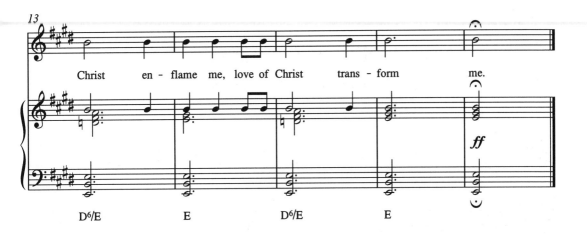

Christ en - flame me, love of Christ trans - form me.

ff

D⁶/E   E   D⁶/E   E

2. Word of Christ instruct me,
   prayer of Christ enrich me,
   work of Christ inspire me,
   light of Christ shine through me.

3. Cross of Christ redeem me,
   pain of Christ be in me,
   bread of Christ sustain me,
   fire of Christ enflame me.

4. Breath of Christ flow in me,
   strength of Christ support me,
   joy of Christ uplift me,
   love of Christ transform me.

5. Peace of Christ surround me,
   light of Christ shine through me,
   fire of Christ enflame me,
   love of Christ transform me.

VOCAL VARIATIONS
MIXED VOICES

Verses 1 and 4

S A

1. Life of Christ re - new me, way of Christ dir - ect me, truth of
4. Breath of Christ flow in me, strength of Christ sup - port me, joy of

T B

Christ re - store me, peace of Christ sur - round me.
Christ up - lift me, love of Christ trans - form me.

Last time

Soprano Descant

p *cresc. al fine*

Ah,

p *cresc. al fine*

5. Peace of Christ sur - round me, light of Christ shine through me, fire of

p *cresc. al fine*

p *cresc. al fine*

Christ en - flame me, love of Christ trans - form me.

Optional Verse 2 for Unaccompanied Women's Voices

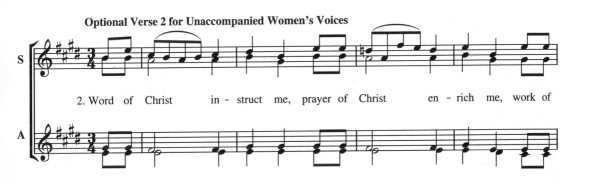

S

2. Word of Christ in - struct me, prayer of Christ en - rich me, work of

A

Christ in - spire me, light of Christ shine through me.

Optional Verse 3 for Unaccompanied Men's Voices

3. Cross of Christ re - deem me, pain of Christ be in me, bread of Christ sus - tain me, fire of Christ en - flame me.

Soprano Descant

4. Breath of Christ flow in me, strength of Christ sup -

port me, joy of Christ up - lift me, love of Christ trans - form me.

INSTRUMENTAL PARTS

C INSTRUMENTS

Variation 1:
Duet for C Instruments

Variation 2:
Duet for C Instruments

Variation 3

Final Variation: Flutes or Violins

Final Variation: Oboe

Bb INSTRUMENTS

Variation 1

Final Variation: Trumpet

Final Variation: Clarinet

BASS CLEF INSTRUMENTS

Basso continuo

Accompaniment to Verses 1 and 4

Accompaniment to Unaccompanied Men's Verse
Duet for Bass clef Instruments

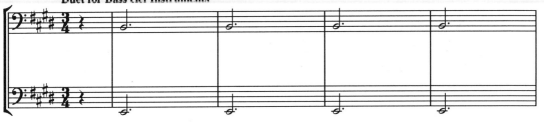

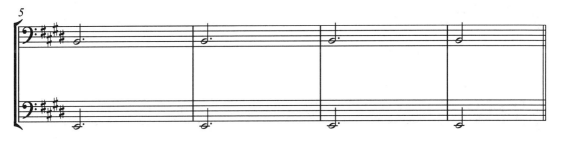

Final Variation
Duet for Bass clef Instruments

TV
131 → Parliament Channel

June
0203 759
5973

John. Bosher @ yahoo.co.uk